Vahe Bedrosian

maggot pie with tiger piss

Maggot Pie with Tiger Piss by Vahe Bedrosian
Self-Published, 2014, 1st Edition
Original art copyright @ 2014 by Vahe Bedrosian
All rights reserved
ISBN-13: 978-0-9906762-0-1
Printed in the United States of America
by CreateSpace, an Amazon.com Company

to my mother who showed me grace

¡ sᴉɥꓕ ¡ ʇɐɥꓕ ʇoN

¡ sᴉɥꓕ

Invitation

come to my scaffolds and cross the sides

I have
balloons and whores and dice
we'll speak of this
and argue that
the newest words for dreams of rats
we'll split the world
in This ! Not That !

they're safe to board like anchored ships
on windless seas of satin sheets
drenched in perfume
from flasks of piss
and wasted nights

I'll bring the clowns
and bags of hash
we'll speak of this
and argue that
the newest words for dreams of rats
we'll split the world
in This ! Not That !

they're safe to watch
the thieves and damned
killers for gain ready to fight
we'll start a war
and bet on sides ; who lives, who dies.

we'll drink champagne,
the band will play
we'll speak of this
and argue that
the newest words for dreams of rats
we'll split the world
in This ! Not That !

come to the edge
let's watch them die
through frames of legs
coiled serpents tight
around their prey in full delight

let's throw the dice:
you're now *a* This !:   your piss is wine
the hungry children ?
they live ?
they die ?
no one will know
they do not count, they are *a* Not That !

Not That !   This !

Contents

Moon Dance

they suck then spit
in mixing pots of maggot wings
then spit some more and stir till's fried
a pinch of sperm, a dead rat's ass

the pie is done

then's time to feast
then's crawl and hump
                    they moo like cows
they moon the moon until she runs
they gas the night with maggot fart
and rape her with their knives

Not That !   This !

Maggot Pie with Tiger Piss

sometimes at night
from gas lit starless streets
you can see
the wretched and the meek
crawling to board the deck
of some old merchant ship

they chew the wood of piss filled boards
the piss of captured tigers
with toothless mouthts
                            they suck then spit
in mixing pots of maggot wings
then spit some more and stir till's fried
a pinch of sperm, a dead rat's ass

the pie is done

then's time to feast
then's crawl and hump
                            they moo like cows
they moon the moon until she runs
they gas the night with maggot fart
and rape her with their knives

                   Requiem aeternam dona eis, Domine
Grant Her eternal rest, O Lord
                 et lux perpetua lucet eis.
and let perpetual light shine upon Her.
                   Requiem aeternam dona eis, Domine
Grant Her eternal rest, O Lord
                 et lux perpetua lucet eis.
and let perpetual light shine upon Her.
                   Requiem aeternam dona eis, Domine
Grant Her eternal rest, O Lord

M 20: Like **it's posted on my page**   how to crawl   and masturbate
M 21: Like   on CNN and Fox   it is the new thing
M 22: Like   and MSNBC   **the spirit of the age**
M 23: Like   on all the channels   it is the new thing   the planet must be saved
M 24: Like   I saw you on TV   we burned a lot of books
M 25: Like   a record on Twitter
M 26: Like   you are so hot
M 27: Like   **no myths no dreams no heroes**   the planet must be saved
M 28: Like   **it's posted on my page**   **the Sun will burn your eyes**   the planet must be saved
M 29: Like   the planet must be saved
M 30: Like   *there is a party in the tunnel: y'all crawl in for drinks and pie*   the planet must be saved

Mr. X shared a link: *no more boring art*

1,000,000 likes   30 comments

M 1: Like   wit is distilled knowledge   very witty   **the planet must be saved**
M 2: Like   **I like it 100 proof**   **bathe him in wit:100 proof wit**
M 3: Like be witty be immortal !   so witty   100 proof wit
M 4: Like   the old man is a witless bore   LOL   so witty !
M 5: Like   **I know him from the streets**   very witty
M 6: Like   LOL   100 proof   burn the lice   bathe him in wit
M 7: Like   **his stench is a bother**   100 proof wit
M 8: Like   3D-HD   a boring dirty bother   **bathe him in wit**
M 9: Like   LOL   that will burn the lice
M 10: Like   that's witty
M 11: Like   so wit**ty**
M 12: Like   knowledge is mortal   **remove the stupid stench**   the planet must be saved
M 13: Like   wit is immortal   **remove the boring stench**   the planet must be saved
M 14: Like   **Breaking News the Pope will come !**   **remove the dirty stench**   the planet must be saved
M 15: Like   isn't she is hot
M 16: Like   **it's in the news**   **she is a witty fuck**
M 17: Like   **on all the channels**   never dull
M 18: Like   on Facebook   I don't give a fuck   the planet must be saved
M 19: Like so honored I was invited ! do you like my ass   just pay the price   the planet must be saved
M 20: Like   **it's posted on my page**   how to crawl   and masturbate
M 21: Like   on CNN and Fox   it is the new thing
M 22: Like   and MSNBC   **the spirit of the age**
M 23: Like   on all the channels   it is the new thing   the planet must be saved
M 24: Like   I saw you on TV   we burned a lot of books
M 25: Like   a record on Twitter
M 26: Like   you are so hot
M 27: Like   **no myths no dreams no heroes**   the planet must be saved
M 28: Like   **it's posted on my page**   **the Sun will burn your eyes**   the planet must be saved
M 29: Like   the planet must be saved
M 30: Like   *there is a party in the tunnel: y'all crawl in for drinks and pie*   the planet must be saved

Mr. X shared a link: *no more boring art*

1,000,000 likes   30 comments

M 1: Like   wit is distilled knowledge   very witty   **the planet must be saved**
M 2: Like   **I like it 100 proof**   **bathe him in wit:100 proof wit**
M 3: Like be witty be immortal !   so witty   100 proof wit
M 4: Like   the old man is a witless bore   LOL   so witty !
M 5: Like   **I know him from the streets**   very witty
M 6: Like   LOL   100 proof   burn the lice   bathe him in wit

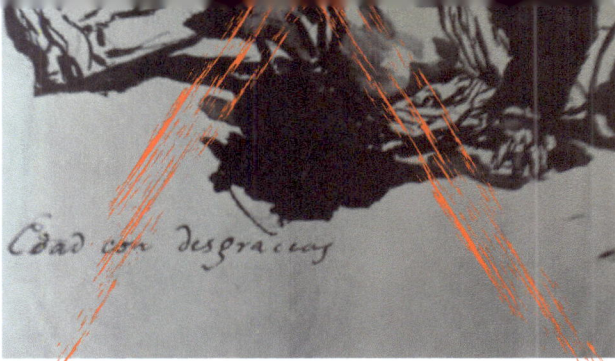

Not That !

This !

very witty !

No More Boring Art

are'nt I witty

10101111001001101010010101001011001
10101111001001101010010101001011001
10101111001001101010010101001011001

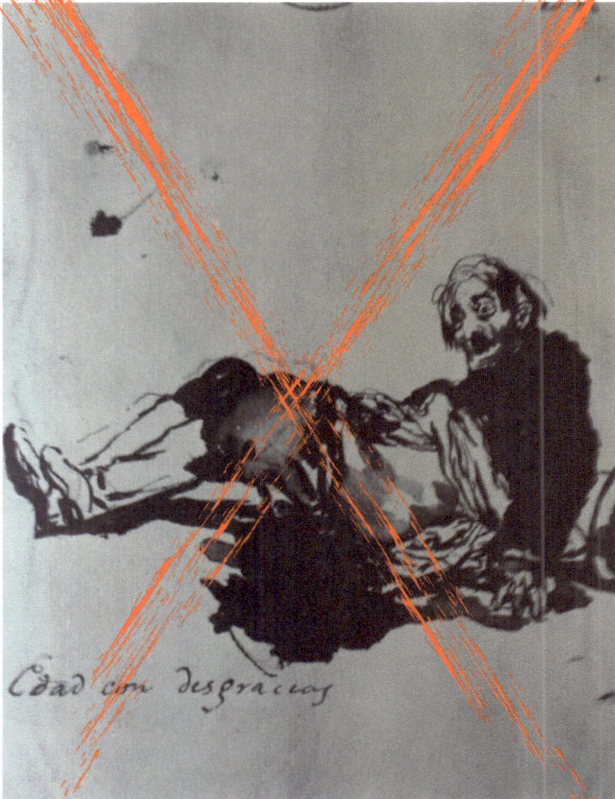

very witty !

Not That !

This !

*Robot Chorus
(with Tenor Solo)*

No More Boring Art

are'nt I witty

10101111001001101010010101001011001

Manifesto a civilized *Manifesto* a civilized *Manifesto* a civilized

M 19: Like   so honored I was invited ! do you like my ass   **pay up**   the planet must be saved
M 20: Like   **it's posted on my page**   it's dance   the planet must be saved
M 21: Like   on CNN and Fox   it's fuck   she's on my page the planet must be saved
M 22: Like   and MSNBC   let's fuck   the planet must be saved
M 23: Like   on all the channels   it's dance   the planet must be saved
M 24: Like   **I saw you on TV**   let's chat   the planet must be saved
M 25: Like   a record on Twitter   it's chat   the planet must be saved
M 26: Like   **you are so hot**   it's posted on my page   let's fuck   the planet must be saved
M 27: Like   **no myths no dreams no heroes**   let's fuck   **the planet must be saved**
M 28: Like   **CRAWL !**   the planet must be saved
M 29: Like   the Sun can burn your eyes   **the planet must be saved**
M 30: Like   *there is a party in the tunnel: y'all crawl in for soup and pie*

she's
twitting
now

Mr. X shared a link: *no myths no dreams no heroes*

1,000,000 likes   30 comments

selfies
from Cannes,
tempting the Sun,

M 1: Like   **no heroes !**   1000011 1010010 1000001 1010111 **1001100**   *on a*   the planet must be saved
M 2: Like   we can buy soldiers   no dreams   no myths   *tall ship*
M 3: Like   heroes are trouble   no dreams   no dreams   *heading*
M 4: Like   all myths are lies   no dreams   no heroes   *due East*   the planet must be saved
M 5: Like   **no myths**   , no lies. we can buy soldiers   **no myths !**   *to star*   the planet must be saved
M 6: Like   we can buy soldiers   **dreams are expensive**   the planet must be saved
M 7: Like   **CRAWL   it's safe in the tunnel**   *crawl*   *for men*   the planet must be saved
M 8: Like   no dreams   *, and boys*   the planet must be saved
M 9: Like   no myths   **no dreams**   *alike.*   **the planet must be saved**
M 10: Like   **no dreams**   **let's chat**   the planet must be saved
M 11: Like   we can buy soldiers   lay down   *oh my !*   the planet must be saved
M 12: Like   **CRAWL**   **look down**   *what ass !*   the planet must be saved
M 13: Like   it's the new thing   get down   *my god !*   the planet must be saved
M 14: Like   **no heroes !**   **lay down**   *she's hot !*   the planet must be saved
M 15: Like   we can buy soldiers   look down   the planet must be saved
M 16: Like   **CRAWL**   it's in the news   **get down**   *a*   the planet must be saved
M 17: Like   **on all the channels**   lay down   the planet must be saved
M 18: Like   on Facebook   **let's chat**   *sailor's*   the planet must be saved
M 19: Like   so honored I was invited ! do you like my ass   **pay up**   *whore*   **the planet must be saved**
M 20: Like   **it's posted on my page**   it's dance   *in Amsterdam*   the planet must be saved
M 21: Like   on CNN and Fox   it's fuck   she's on my page   **the planet must be saved**
M 22: Like   and MSNBC   let's fuck   the planet must be saved
M 23: Like   on all the channels   it's dance   *a*   the planet must be saved
M 24: Like   **I saw you on TV**   let's chat   *sailor's*   the planet must be saved
M 25: Like   a record on Twitter   it's chat   the planet must be saved
M 26: Like   **you are so hot**   it's posted on my page   let's fuck   the planet must be saved
M 27: Like   **no myths no dreams no heroes**   let's fuck   **the planet must be saved**
M 28: Like   **CRAWL !**   the planet must be saved
M 29: Like   the Sun can burn your eyes   **the planet must be saved**
M 30: Like   *there is a party in the tunnel: y'all crawl in for soup and pie*

oh my !
what ass !
my god !
she's hot !

Mr. X shared a link: *no myths no dreams no heroes*

1,000,000 likes   30 comments

M 1: Like   **no heroes !**   1000011 1010010 1000001 1010111 **1001100**   *ooh ! what a fuck !*   the planet must be saved
M 2: Like   we can buy soldiers   no dreams   no myths   *for sale to men*
M 3: Like   heroes are trouble   no dreams   no dreams   *, and boys*
M 4: Like   all myths are lies   no dreams   no heroes   *alike.*
M 5: Like   **no myths**   , no lies. we can buy soldiers   **no myths !**   the planet must be saved
M 6: Like   we can buy soldiers   **dreams are expensive**   the planet must be saved
M 7: Like   **CRAWL   it's safe in the tunnel**   *crawl*   the planet must be saved
M 8: Like   no dreams   the planet must be saved

crawl !

Not That !

This !

1000011 1010010 1000001 1010111 1001100
1000011 1010010 1000001 1010111 1001100
1000011 1010010 1000001 1010111 1001100
1000011 1010010 1000001 1010111 1001100
1000011 1010010 1000001 1010111 1001100
1000011 1010010 1000001 1010111 1001100
1000011 1010010 1000001 1010111 1001100

CRAWL !

Not That !

This !

Robot Chorus
(Falsetto Children Voices)

1010111 1001100 0100001 1000011 101
01 1000011 1010010 1000001

No heroes ! No myths No dreams No heroes !

M 19: Like   so honored I was invited ! **let's fuck**   ***and fuck***
M 20: Like   *and whisper Hallelujah*
M 21: Like   on CNN and Fox
M 22: Like   and MSNBC   **CRAWL**
M 23: Like   on all the channels CRAWL !   it's the new thing   the planet must be saved
M 24: Like   I saw you on TV
M 25: Like   a record on Twitter
M 26: Like   your ass is hot
M 27: Like   it's posted on my page
M 28: Like
M 29: Like   the Sun will burn your eyes
M 30: Like   *there is a party*   Come crawl inside my cup !

Mr. X shared a link: *the seduction of the wild*

1,000,000 likes   30 comments

M 1: Like   look down the Sun will burn your eyes
M 2: Like ***don't fly***   *lay down   !*
M 3: Like   *don't fly*   *you'll burn*   *look down   !*
M 4: Like *look down   the Sun will burn your eyes*
M 5: Like   ***don't fly***   *my lips are wet*
M 6: Like   ***don't fly***   *my breasts are young*
M 7: Like   *the arms are stretched*
M 8: Like   ***look down***   *my legs apart*
M 9: Like   ***my mouth***
M 10: Like   *into the cup of my hips*
M 11: Like   *open ready to drink*
M 12: Like   ***Press in*** *and taste the cup*
M 13: Like   ***Come in !***
M 14: Like   ***I'll teach you Hallelujah***
M 15: Like
M 16: Like it's in the news   Shamhat a temple prostitute
M 17: Like   on all the channels   *there in town*
M 18: Like   on Facebook   *we drink*
M 19: Like so honored I was invited ! **let's fuck**   ***and fuck***
M 20: Like   *and whisper Hallelujah*
M 21: Like   on CNN and Fox
M 22: Like   and MSNBC   **CRAWL**
M 23: Like   on all the channels CRAWL !   it's the new thing   the planet must be saved
M 24: Like   I saw you on TV
M 25: Like   a record on Twitter
M 26: Like   your ass is hot
M 27: Like   it's posted on my page
M 28: Like
M 29: Like   the Sun will burn your eyes
M 30: Like   *there is a party*   Come crawl inside my cup !

Mr. X shared a link: *the seduction of the wild*

1,000,000 likes   30 comments

M 1: Like   look down the Sun will burn your eyes
M 2: Like ***don't fly***   *lay down   !*
M 3: Like   *don't fly*   *you'll burn*   *look down   !*
M 4: Like *look down   the Sun will burn your eyes*
M 5: Like   ***don't fly***   *my lips are wet*
M 6: Like   ***don't fly***   *my breasts are young*
M 7: Like   *the arms are stretched*
M 8: Like   ***look down***   *my legs apart*
M 9: Like   ***my mouth***

Not That !   This !

Not That !   This !

001101... (binary rows)

1010111 1001100 0100001 1000011 101

001 1000011 1010010 1000001

000111 1001100 0100001

1001100 0100001 100

WL ! CRAWL ! C

Robot Chorus
(Soprano Falsetto Voice)

1010111 1001100 0100001 1000011 101
01 1000011 1010010 1000001

! Enjoy the pleasures of the town !

8

M 19: Like   so honored I was invited ! you can have my ass   crawling's badass   the planet must be saved
M 20: Like   it's posted on my page   the planet must be saved
M 21: Like   on CNN and Fox   Such a great Artist
M 22: Like   and MSNBC   The Spirit of the Age
M 23: Like   on all the channels   **CRAWL !**   it's the new thing   the planet must be saved
M 24: Like   I saw you on TV
M 25: Like   a record on Twitter
M 26: Like   **you are so hot**   the planet must be saved
M 27: Like   *there is a party in the tunnel: y'all crawl in He'll play your ass*   the planet must be saved
M 28: Like   it's posted on my page   **the Sun will burn your eyes**   the planet must be saved
M 29: Like   3D-HD   the planet must be saved
M 30: Like   *there is a party in the tunnel: y'all crawl in for piss and pie*   the planet must be saved

Mr. X shared a link: *CRAWL !*

1,000,000 likes   30 comments

M 1: Like   I loved His new show   the planet must be saved
M 2: Like   CRAWLING   the planet must be saved
M 3: Like   the promise of the town   the planet must be saved
M 4: Like   ZEITGEIST   the comfort of the many   the planet must be saved
M 5: Like   **such a great Artist**   the planet must be saved
M 6: Like   I missed you at the party   the planet must be saved
M 7: Like   the planet must be saved
M 8: Like   all in 3D   ZEITGEIST   the planet must be saved
M 9: Like   LOL   the planet must be saved
M 10: Like   the Sun will burn your eyes   look down   the planet must be saved
M 11: Like   the Sun will burn your eyes   lay down   the planet must be saved
M 12: Like   **CRAWL**   stay down   the planet must be saved
M 13: Like   crawling's badass   the planet must be saved
M 14: Like   crawling's badass   the planet must be saved
M 15: Like   **isn't she hot**   the planet must be saved
M 16: Like   it's in the news   the planet must be saved
M 17: Like   a Crawl'n Fuck delight   watch us in 3D   the planet must be saved
M 18: Like   on Facebook   crawling's badass   the planet must be saved
M 19: Like   so honored I was invited ! you can have my ass   crawling's badass   the planet must be saved
M 20: Like   it's posted on my page   the planet must be saved
M 21: Like   on CNN and Fox   Such a great Artist
M 22: Like   and MSNBC   The Spirit of the Age
M 23: Like   on all the channels   **CRAWL !**   it's the new thing   the planet must be saved
M 24: Like   I saw you on TV
M 25: Like   a record on Twitter
M 26: Like   **you are so hot**   the planet must be saved
M 27: Like   *there is a party in the tunnel: y'all crawl in He'll play your ass*   the planet must be saved
M 28: Like   it's posted on my page   **the Sun will burn your eyes**   the planet must be saved
M 29: Like   3D-HD   the planet must be saved
M 30: Like   *there is a party in the tunnel: y'all crawl in for piss and pie*   the planet must be saved

Mr. X shared a link: *CRAWL !*

1,000,000 likes   30 comments

M 1: Like   I loved His new show   the planet must be saved
M 2: Like   CRAWLING   the planet must be saved
M 3: Like   the promise of the town   the planet must be saved
M 4: Like   ZEITGEIST   the comfort of the many   the planet must be saved
M 5: Like   **such a great Artist**   the planet must be saved
M 6: Like   I missed you at the party   the planet must be saved
M 7: Like   the planet must be saved

1000110011001111011010110000001000010011101000011110110010101110110100010001110110000110101101100

WL ! CRAWL ! C

Not That ! This !

1001100 0100001 1000011 1010010 1000001 1010111 1001100 0100001 1000011 1010010 1000001 1010111 1001100 0100001 1000011 1010010 1000001 1010111 1001100 0100001 1

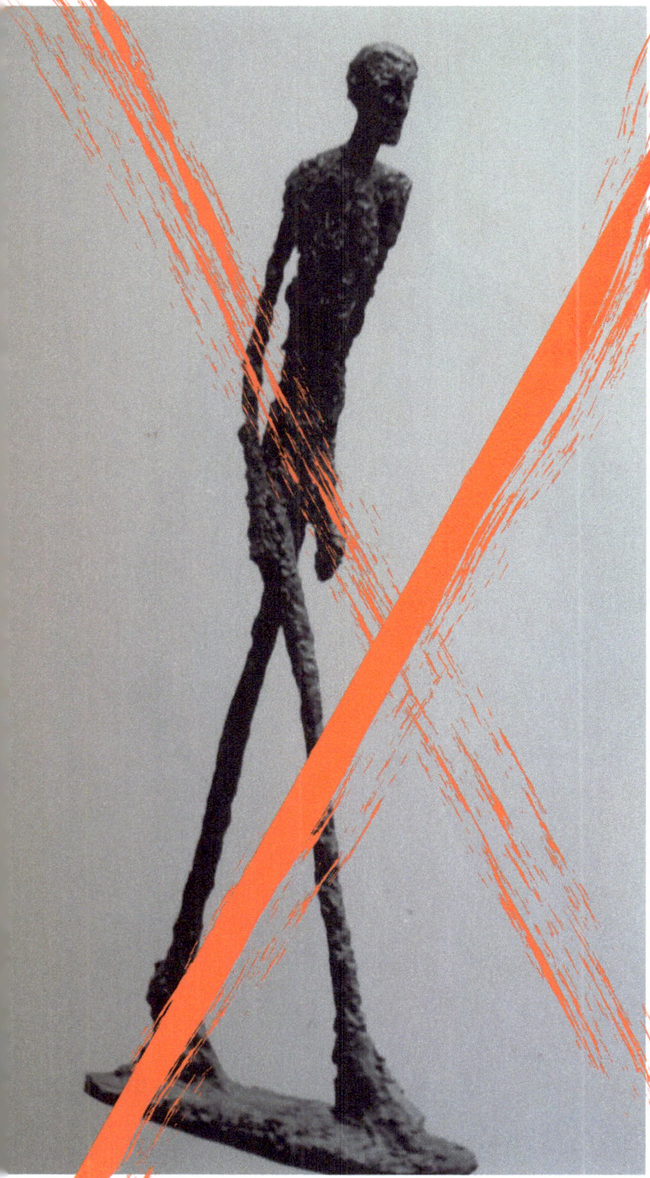

1010010 1000001 1010111 1001100 0100001 1000011 1010010 1000001 1010111 1001100 0100001 1000011 1010010 1000001 1010111 1001100 0

0100001 1000011 1010010 1000001 1010111 1001100 0100001 1000011 1010010 1000001 1010111 1001100 0100001 1000011 1010010 1000001

1000011 1010010 1000001 1010111 1001100 0100001 1000011 1010010 1000001 1010111 1001100 0100001 1000011 101

1000011 1010010 1000001 1010111 1001100 0100001 1000011 1010010 1000001 1010111 1001100 010

1000011 1010010 1000001 1010111 1001100 0100001 1000011 1010010 1000001

1010111 1001100 0100001 1000011 1010010 1000001 1010111 100110

1001100 0100001 1000011 1010010 1000001 1010111 100110

1010111 1001100 0100001 1000011 101

001 1000011 1010010 1000001

000111 1001100 0100001

1001100 0100001 100

WL ! CRAWL ! C

Not That ! This !

Robot Chorus

(Baritone Falsetto Voice)

1010111 1001100 0100001 1000011 101

1010111 1001100 0100001 1000011 101

1100 10000111010010100000110101111001100 1000

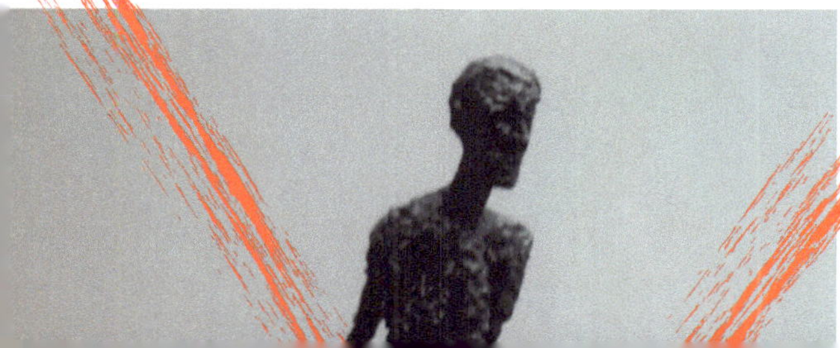

M 21: Like on CNN and Fox — they will be burning books it is the new thing — the planet must be saved
M 22: Like and MSNBC — they will be burning books — the planet must be saved
M 23: Like on all the channels — it is the new thing — the planet must be saved
M 24: Like on TV — we will be burning books — the planet must be saved
M 25: Like a billion on Twitter — a vote for selfie party — it is the new thing — the planet must be saved
M26: Like more every minute there is a party — they will be burning books it is the new thing — the planet must be saved
M27: Like going Downtown there is a party — we will be burning books it is the new thing — the planet must be saved
M28: Like there is a party — we will be burning books it is the new thing — the planet must be saved
M29: Like CNN announced ! — the selfie won ! the selfies won !!!!! — the planet will be saved
M30: Like MSNBC announced ! — the selfie won ! the selfies won !!!!! — the planet will be saved

Mr. X shared a link : *vote for selfie 2014*

1,000,000 likes   30 comments

M 1: Like going Downtown there is a party — a vote for selfie party — it is the new thing — the planet must be saved
M 2: Like I am too there is a party — they will be burning books it is the new thing — the planet must be saved
M 3: Like going Downtown there is a party — a vote for selfie party — it is the new thing — the planet must be saved
M 4: Like — it is the new thing — the planet must be saved
M 5: Like it is a nice day there is a party — a vote for selfie party — it is the new thing — the planet must be saved
M 6: Like sunny there is a party — they will be burning books — the planet must be saved
M 7: Like no rain there is a party — a vote for selfie party — the planet must be saved
M 8: Like He will come — they will be burning books it is the new thing — the planet must be saved
M 9: Like He might be Downtown — a vote for selfie party — the planet must be saved
M 10: Like it was announced there is a party — they will be burning books — the planet must be saved
M 11: Like — they will be burning books is that your girlfriend — the planet must be saved
M 12: Like — they will be burning books from a site — the planet must be saved
M 13: Like — they will be burning books she's hot — the planet must be saved
M 14: Like there was a sighting — they will be burning books we tweet — the planet must be saved
M 15: Like it was confirmed — they will be burning books she's hot — the planet must be saved
M 16: Like Breaking News — they will be burning books — the planet must be saved
M 17: Like on all the channels — they will be burning books it is the new thing — the planet must be saved
M 18: Like on Facebook — a vote for selfie party — 3D-HD — the planet must be saved
M 19: Like I am going I was invited — they will be burning books highdef — the planet must be saved
M 20: Like I am too there is a party — they will be burning books — HD — the planet must be saved
M 21: Like on CNN and Fox — they will be burning books it is the new thing — the planet must be saved
M 22: Like and MSNBC — they will be burning books — the planet must be saved
M 23: Like on all the channels — it is the new thing — the planet must be saved
M 24: Like on TV — we will be burning books — the planet must be saved
M 25: Like a billion on Twitter — a vote for selfie party — it is the new thing — the planet must be saved
M26: Like more every minute there is a party — they will be burning books it is the new thing — the planet must be saved
M27: Like going Downtown there is a party — we will be burning books it is the new thing — the planet must be saved
M28: Like there is a party — we will be burning books it is the new thing — the planet must be saved
M29: Like CNN announced ! — the selfie won ! the selfies won !!!!! — the planet will be saved
M30: Like MSNBC announced ! — the selfie won ! the selfies won !!!!! — the planet will be saved

Mr. X shared a link : *vote for selfie 2014*

1,000,000 likes   30 comments

M 1: Like going Downtown there is a party — a vote for selfie party — it is the new thing — the planet must be saved
M 2: Like I am too there is a party — they will be burning books it is the new thing — the planet must be saved
M 3: Like going Downtown there is a party — a vote for selfie party — it is the new thing — the planet must be saved
M 4: Like — it is the new thing — the planet must be saved
M 5: Like it is a nice day there is a party — a vote for selfie party — it is the new thing — the planet must be saved
M 6: Like sunny there is a party — they will be burning books — the planet must be saved

Selfie !

Selfie !

Selfie !

Long !
Live !
The
Selfie !

Long
Live
The
Selfie !

Long
Live
The
Selfie

Long
Live
The
Selfie

Long
Live
The
Selfie !

Long
Live
The
Selfie

Long !
Live !
The
Selfie !

Long
Live
The
Selfie !

Selfie

Long
Live
The
Selfie

Long Live The Selfie Long Live The Selfie

2014 Vote for Selfie 2014 ! Vote !

M 20: Like	there is a party — they will be burning books		the planet must be saved
M 21: Like	on CNN and Fox — burning books for soup		the planet must be saved
M 22: Like	and MSNBC — burning books		the planet must be saved
M 23: Like	on all the channels in 3D		the planet must be saved
M 24: Like	on TV — we will be burning books		the planet must be saved
M 25: Like	a billion on Twitter — eating soup and pie		the planet must be saved
M 26: Like	there is a party — they will be burning books		the planet must be saved
M 27: Like	in Downtown there is a party — we will be burning books		the planet must be saved
M 28: Like	there is a party — we will be burning books		the planet must be saved
M 29: Like	**there is a war you know** turn in your books for soup	the soldiers must be fed	the planet must be saved
M 30: Like		**it's decadent to think**	the planet must be saved

Mr. X shared a link : *turn in your books for soup*

1,000,000 likes   30 comments

M 1: Like	**there is a war you know** turn in your books for soup	**the soldiers must be fed**	turn in your books for soup
M 2: Like		it's decadent to think	
M 3: Like		to think like a child	
M 4: Like	turn in your books for soup it's treasonous to dream	there is a war you know	turn in your books for soup
M 5: Like		it's decadent to dream	
M 6: Like		to dream like a child	
M 7: Like	there is a war you know turn in your books for soup	the soldiers must be fed	turn in your books for soup
M 8: Like		it's decadent to play	
M 9: Like		to play like a child	
M 10: Like	turn in your books for soup it's treasonous to dream	the soldiers must be fed	the planet must be saved
M 11: Like	there is a war you know turn in your books for soup	the soldiers must be fed	the planet must be saved
M 12: Like			the planet must be saved
M 13: Like		they're giving soup for books	the planet must be saved
M 14: Like	there was a sighting		
M 15: Like	it was confirmed — in Downtown		
M 16: Like	Breaking News — they're burning books for soup		
M 17: Like	on all the channels — they're burning books for soup		
M 18: Like	on Facebook		
M 19: Like	I was invited — to piss and have some pie		the planet must be saved
M 20: Like	there is a party — they will be burning books		the planet must be saved
M 21: Like	on CNN and Fox — burning books for soup		the planet must be saved
M 22: Like	and MSNBC — burning books		the planet must be saved
M 23: Like	on all the channels in 3D		the planet must be saved
M 24: Like	on TV — we will be burning books		the planet must be saved
M 25: Like	a billion on Twitter — eating soup and pie		the planet must be saved
M 26: Like	there is a party — they will be burning books		the planet must be saved
M 27: Like	in Downtown there is a party — we will be burning books		the planet must be saved
M 28: Like	there is a party — we will be burning books		the planet must be saved
M 29: Like	**there is a war you know** turn in your books for soup	the soldiers must be fed	the planet must be saved
M 30: Like		**it's decadent to think**	the planet must be saved

Mr. X shared a link : *turn in your books for soup*

1,000,000 likes   30 comments

M 1: Like	**there is a war you know** turn in your books for soup	**the soldiers must be fed**	turn in your books for soup
M 2: Like		it's decadent to think	
M 3: Like		to think like a child	
M 4: Like	turn in your books for soup it's treasonous to dream	there is a war you know	turn in your books for soup
M 5: Like		it's decadent to dream	
M 6: Like		to dream like a child	
M 7: Like	there is a war you know turn in your books for soup	the soldiers must be fed	turn in your books for soup

Not That !

This !

Not That !

This !

the People's Choice !

the People's Choice !

! the People's Choice !

Paul Klee Notebooks Volume 1 The thinking eye

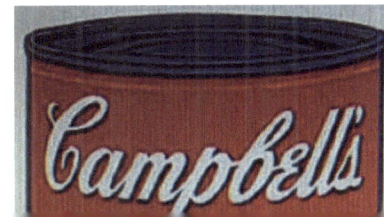

Campbell's CONDENSED TOMATO SOUP

TOMATO SOUP

Paul Klee Notebooks Volume 1 The thinking eye

Campbell's

ra ra ra

bra bra bra

hey peasant !

what an ass

that's not how you dance

boo boo boo

ra ra ra

a brute

M 6: Like
M 5: Like
M 4: Like
M 3: Like
M 2: Like
M 1: Like

1,000,000 likes   25 comments

Mr. X shared a link : a peasant's dance

a brute

no wit

a peasant

fuck off

an ass

you brute

boo boo boo

ra ra ra

bra bra bra

so offensive
fuck off go home
go home fuck off

boo

asshole

that's not a dance

o ha ha

bra bra bra

ra ra ra

hey peasant !

what an ass

that's not how you dance

M 25: Like
M 24: Like
M 23: Like
M 22: Like

M 21: Like

M 20: Like
M 19: Like
M 18: Like
M 17: Like
M 16: Like
M 15: Like
M 14: Like
M 13: Like
M 12: Like
M 11: Like
M 10: Like
M 9: Like
M 8: Like
M 7: Like
M 6: Like
M 5: Like
M 4: Like
M 3: Like
M 2: Like
M 1: Like

1,000,000 likes   25 comments

Mr. X shared a link : a peasant's dance

M 25: Like
M 24: Like
M 23: Like
M 22: Like

M 21: Like

M 20: Like

asshole
bra bra bra
o ha ha
ra ra ra
boo boo boo
go home
bra bra bra
o ha ha

that's not a dance
o o ha ha

o bra bra bra
ra ra ra
go home

what an ass
hey peasant !
that's not how you dance
that's not how you dance

hey peasant
bra bra bra
ra ra ra

boo
so offensive
fuck off
go home fuck off
bra bra bra
ra ra ra
boo boo boo
ra ra ra
asshole
fuck off
o ha ha

what an ass
hey peasant !
that's not how you dance
a brute
no wit
a peasant
an ass
fuck off
you brute
go home
bra bra bra

Not That !

This !

be civilized ! be civilized ! be civilized ! be civilized !

1010111 1001100 0100001 1000011 101
001 1000011 1010010 1000001
000111 1001100 0100001
1001100 0100001 100

WL ! CRAWL ! C

don't be a peasant !

Not That !

This !

*Robot Chorus
(All voices)*

1010111 1001100 0100001 1000011 1C1
01 1000011 1010010 1000001

M 21: Like   I Love Piss !
M 22: Like   I dont't understand!   **we chased the moon away,**   **I don't understand ! lusts, thrilling and sweet ?**
M 23: Like   **he's a fool**
M 24: Like   **there is no moon**
M 25: Like   **just gas lamps**
M 26: Like   there is no looking up   he must be a fool !
M 27: Like   **we crawl looking down**   we suck and sip each other's   piss,   **we fuck on demand**
M 28: Like   **he's a fool**   **: we fuck on demand**
M 29: Like   what does he mean   **lusts, thrilling and sweet ?**   a decadent fool
M 30: Like   **what does he mean**   I don't understand,   he must be a fool.   **Pierrot's a fool, a dangerous fool !**

Mr. X shared a link : *piss's better than moon wine*

1,000,000 likes   30 comments

M 1: Like   I don't understand !   **Drunk with Moonlight**   he must be a fool   **Pierrot the Fool !**
M 2: Like   what does this mean   a dangerous fool
M 3: Like   t'is shit !   "The wine that one drinks with one's eyes
M 4: Like   I say   Is poured down in waves by the moon at night,
M 5: Like   stupid shit !   And a spring tide overflows
M 6: Like   what does that mean   The silent horizon
M 7: Like   I don't understand   **the moon, she's run away**
M 8: Like   what does this mean   Lusts, thrilling and sweet,
M 9: Like   such shit   Float numberless through the waters !
M 10: Like   holy shit !   The wine that one drinks with one's eyes
M 11: Like   what does he mean   Is poured down in waves by the moon at night,
M 12: Like   I don't understand   **the moon, she's run away**
M 13: Like   what does this mean   The poet, urged on by his devotions,
M 14: Like   what does he mean   Becomes intoxicated with the sacred beverage;
M 15: Like   so lame   Enraptured, he turns toward heaven
M 16: Like   no wit   His head, and, staggering, sucks and sips
M 17: Like   just crap !   The wine that one drinks with one's eyes "   Pierrot's a fool !
M 18: Like   such crap !   wine
M 19: Like   holy crap !   **I don't understand ! poured from the moon ?**
M 20: Like   we drink piss
M 21: Like   I Love Piss !
M 22: Like   I dont't understand!   **we chased the moon away,**   **I don't understand ! lusts, thrilling and sweet ?**
M 23: Like   **he's a fool**
M 24: Like   **there is no moon**
M 25: Like   **just gas lamps**
M 26: Like   there is no looking up   he must be a fool !
M 27: Like   **we crawl looking down**   we suck and sip each other's   piss,   **we fuck on demand**
M 28: Like   **he's a fool**   **: we fuck on demand**
M 29: Like   what does he mean   **lusts, thrilling and sweet ?**   a decadent fool
M 30: Like   **what does he mean**   I don't understand,   he must be a fool.   **Pierrot's a fool, a dangerous fool !**

Mr. X shared a link : *piss's better than moon wine*

1,000,000 likes   30 comments

M 1: Like   I don't understand !   **Drunk with Moonlight**   he must be a fool   **Pierrot the Fool !**
M 2: Like   what does this mean   a dangerous fool
M 3: Like   t'is shit !   "The wine that one drinks with one's eyes
M 4: Like   I say   Is poured down in waves by the moon at night,
M 5: Like   stupid shit !   And a spring tide overflows
M 6: Like   what does that mean   The silent horizon
M 7: Like   I don't understand   **the moon, she's run away**
M 8: Like   what does this mean   Lusts, thrilling and sweet,
M 9: Like

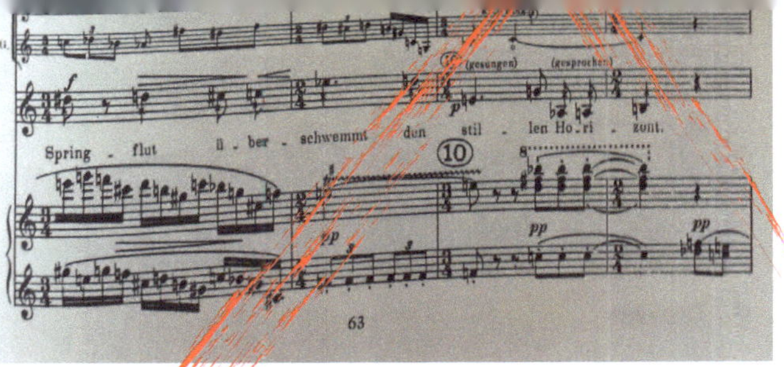

Not That !   This !

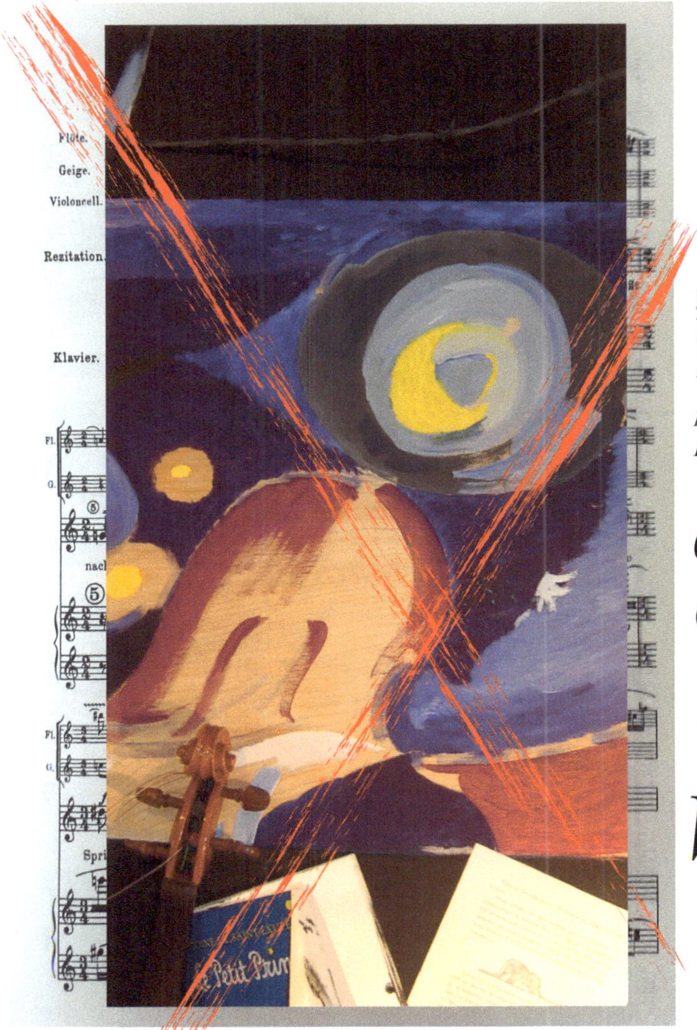

piss's better than moon wine

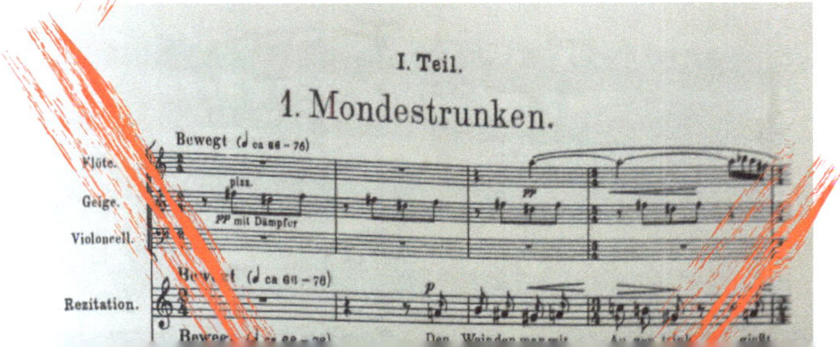

pissdrunk ! *pissdrunk !*

1010111 1001100 0100001 1000011 1010010 1000001 1010111 1001100 0100001 1000011 101

1010111 1001100 0100001 1000011 1010010 1000001 1010111 1001100 0100001 1000011 101

001 1000011 1010010 1000001

CRAWL ! PISS DRUNK

1001100 0100001 10

WL ! CRAWL ! C

Not That !   This !

Robot Chorus

(all falsetto voices)

1010111 1001100 0100001 1000011 101

01 1000011 1010010 1000001

M 21: Like   OMG   congrats   OMG   I touched myself   I touched myself

M 22: Like   OMG   OMG OMG

M 23: Like   OMG   OMG   I touched myself

here's my ass

M 24: Like   OMG   ur so good   congrats congrats

M 25: Like   OMG   love it

M 26: Like   OMG   congrats

I touched myself

M 27: Like   OMG   here's my ass   here's my ass

M 28: Like   OMG

M 29: Like   OMG   congrats   Congrats

M 30: Like   OMG   congrats

Congrats

Mr. X shared a link : my wining selfie / *" selfie with red white and blue "*

1,000,000 likes   30 comments

M 1: Like   OMG   ur so good   OMG

M 2: Like   OMG   I love it   here's my ass

M 3: Like   OMG   congrats

M 4: Like   OMG   here's my ass

M 5: Like   OMG   I touched myself

M 6: Like   OMG   ur so good   I touched myself

I touched myself

M 7: Like   OMG   I touched myself

M 8: Like   OMG   ur so good   here's my ass

M 9: Like   OMG   ur so good

M 10: Like   OMG   love it

M 11: Like   OMG   XOX   OMG

M 12: Like   OMG   congrats congrats

M 13: Like   OMG   ur the best   I touched myself   I touched myself

M 14: Like   OMG   here's my ass   here's my ass

M 15: Like   OMG   here's my ass

M 16: Like   OMG   congrats

M 17: Like   OMG   congrats

M 18: Like   OMG   XOX   I touched myself

M 19: Like   OMG   love it   XXX

M 20: Like   OMG   congrats

M 21: Like   OMG   congrats   OMG   I touched myself   I touched myself

M 22: Like   OMG   OMG OMG

M 23: Like   OMG   OMG   I touched myself

I touched myself

M 24: Like   OMG   ur so good   congrats congrats

M 25: Like   OMG   love it

M 26: Like   OMG   congrats   here's my ass

M 27: Like   OMG   here's my ass

M 28: Like   OMG   Congrats

M 29: Like   OMG   congrats

M 30: Like   OMG   congrats   Congrats

Mr. X shared a link : my wining selfie / *" selfie with red white and blue "*

1,000,000 likes   30 comments

M 1: Like   OMG   ur so good   OMG

M 2: Like   OMG   I love it   here's my ass

M 3: Like   OMG   congrats

M 4: Like   OMG   here's my ass   I touched myself

M 5: Like   OMG   I touched myself

M 6: Like   OMG   ur so good   I touched myself   here's my ass

M 7: Like   OMG   I touched myself

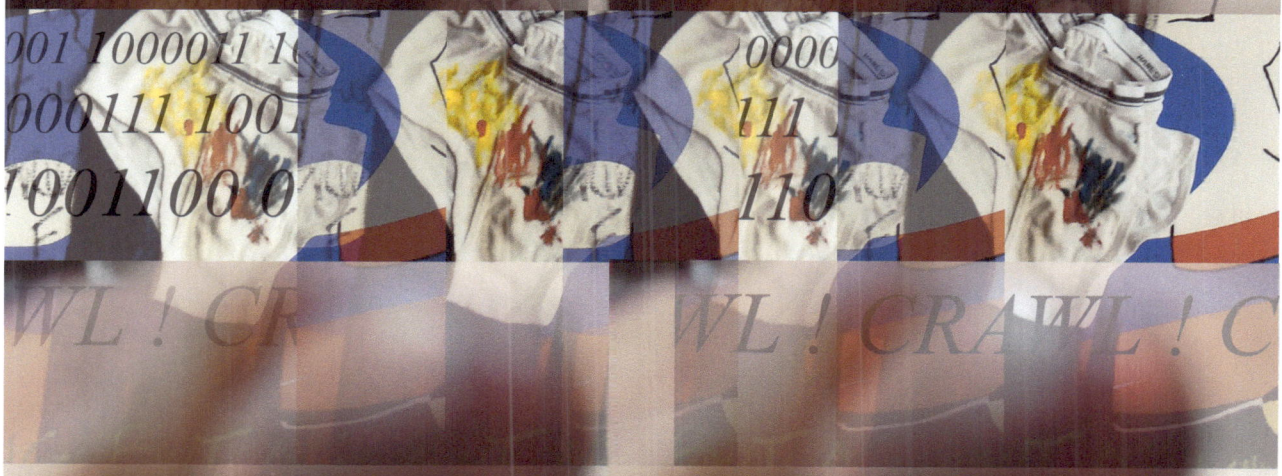

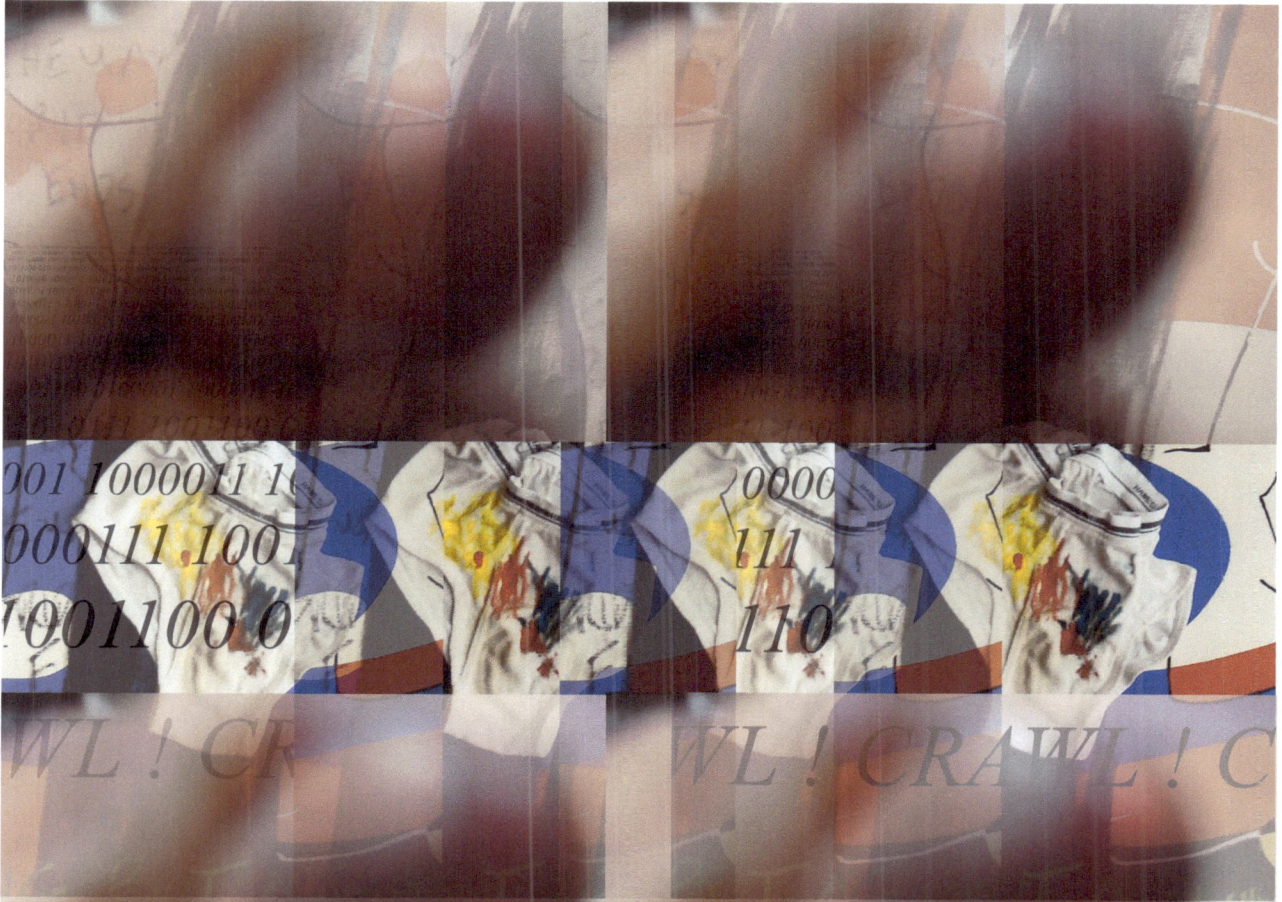

Selfie with red white and blue [19]

red white and blue

20

M 21: Like	kill the priest	kill the priest	kill the priest	kill the priest	kill the priest	kill the priest
M 22: Like	kill the priest	kill the priest	kill the priest	kill the priest	kill the priest	kill the priest
M 23: Like	kill the priest	kill the priest	kill the priest	kill the priest	kill the priest	kill the priest
M 24: Like	kill the priest	kill the priest	kill the priest	kill the priest	kill the priest	kill the priest
M 25: Like	kill the priest	kill the priest	kill the priest	kill the priest	kill the priest	kill the priest
M 26: Like	kill the priest	kill the priest	kill the priest	kill the priest	kill the priest	kill the priest
M 27: Like	kill the priest	kill the priest	kill the priest	kill the priest	kill the priest	kill the priest
M 28: Like	kill the priest	kill the priest	kill the priest	kill the priest	kill the priest	kill the priest
M 29: Like	kill the priest	kill the priest	kill the priest	kill the priest	kill the priest	kill the priest
M 30: Like	kill the priest	kill the priest	kill the priest	kill the priest	kill the priest	kill the priest

Mr. X shared a link : *kill the priest*

1,000,000 likes   30 comments

M 1: Like	kill the priest	kill the priest	kill the priest	kill the priest	kill the priest	kill the priest
M 2: Like	kill the priest	kill the priest	kill the priest	kill the priest	kill the priest	kill the priest
M 3: Like	kill the priest	kill the priest	kill the priest	kill the priest	kill the priest	kill the priest
M 4: Like	kill the priest	kill the priest	kill the priest	kill the priest	kill the priest	kill the priest
M 5: Like	kill the priest	kill the priest	kill the priest	kill the priest	kill the priest	kill the priest
M 6: Like	kill the priest	kill the priest	kill the priest	kill the priest	kill the priest	kill the priest
M 7: Like	kill the priest	kill the priest	kill the priest	kill the priest	kill the priest	kill the priest
M 8: Like	kill the priest	kill the priest	kill the priest	kill the priest	kill the priest	kill the priest
M 9: Like	kill the priest	kill the priest	kill the priest	kill the priest	kill the priest	kill the priest
M 10: Like	kill the priest	kill the priest	kill the priest	kill the priest	kill the priest	kill the priest
M 11: Like	kill the priest	kill the priest	kill the priest	kill the priest	kill the priest	kill the priest
M 12: Like	kill the priest	kill the priest	kill the priest	kill the priest	kill the priest	kill the priest
M 13: Like	kill the priest	kill the priest	kill the priest	kill the priest	kill the priest	kill the priest
M 14: Like	kill the priest	kill the priest	kill the priest	kill the priest	kill the priest	kill the priest
M 15: Like	kill the priest	kill the priest	kill the priest	kill the priest	kill the priest	kill the priest
M 16: Like	kill the priest	kill the priest	kill the priest	kill the priest	kill the priest	kill the priest
M 17: Like	kill the priest	kill the priest	kill the priest	kill the priest	kill the priest	kill the priest
M 18: Like	kill the priest	kill the priest	kill the priest	kill the priest	kill the priest	kill the priest
M 19: Like	kill the priest	kill the priest	kill the priest	kill the priest	kill the priest	kill the priest
M 20: Like	kill the priest	kill the priest	kill the priest	kill the priest	kill the priest	kill the priest
M 21: Like	kill the priest	kill the priest	kill the priest	kill the priest	kill the priest	kill the priest
M 22: Like	kill the priest	kill the priest	kill the priest	kill the priest	kill the priest	kill the priest
M 23: Like	kill the priest	kill the priest	kill the priest	kill the priest	kill the priest	kill the priest
M 24: Like	kill the priest	kill the priest	kill the priest	kill the priest	kill the priest	kill the priest
M 25: Like	kill the priest	kill the priest	kill the priest	kill the priest	kill the priest	kill the priest
M 26: Like	kill the priest	kill the priest	kill the priest	kill the priest	kill the priest	kill the priest
M 27: Like	kill the priest	kill the priest	kill the priest	kill the priest	kill the priest	kill the priest
M 28: Like	kill the priest	kill the priest	kill the priest	kill the priest	kill the priest	kill the priest
M 29: Like	kill the priest	kill the priest	kill the priest	kill the priest	kill the priest	kill the priest
M 30: Like	kill the priest	kill the priest	kill the priest	kill the priest	kill the priest	kill the priest

Mr. X shared a link : *kill the priest*

1,000,000 likes   30 comments

M 1: Like	kill the priest	kill the priest	kill the priest	kill the priest	kill the priest	kill the priest
M 2: Like	kill the priest	kill the priest	kill the priest	kill the priest	kill the priest	kill the priest
M 3: Like	kill the priest	kill the priest	kill the priest	kill the priest	kill the priest	kill the priest
M 4: Like	kill the priest	kill the priest	kill the priest	kill the priest	kill the priest	kill the priest
M 5: Like	kill the priest	kill the priest	kill the priest	kill the priest	kill the priest	kill the priest
M 6: Like	kill the priest	kill the priest	kill the priest	kill the priest	kill the priest	kill the priest
M 7: Like	kill the priest	kill the priest	kill the priest	kill the priest	kill the priest	kill the priest

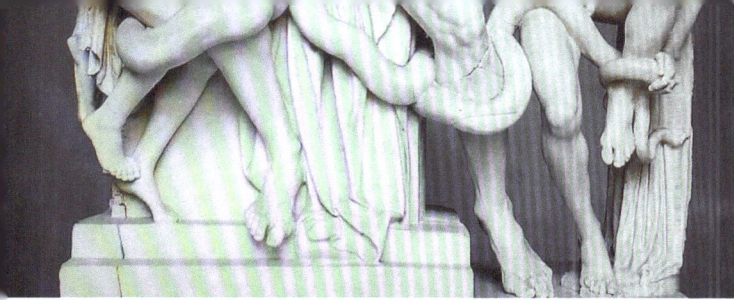

00101110010011001100100110 0100001

Kill !

00101110010011001100100110 0100001

Kill !

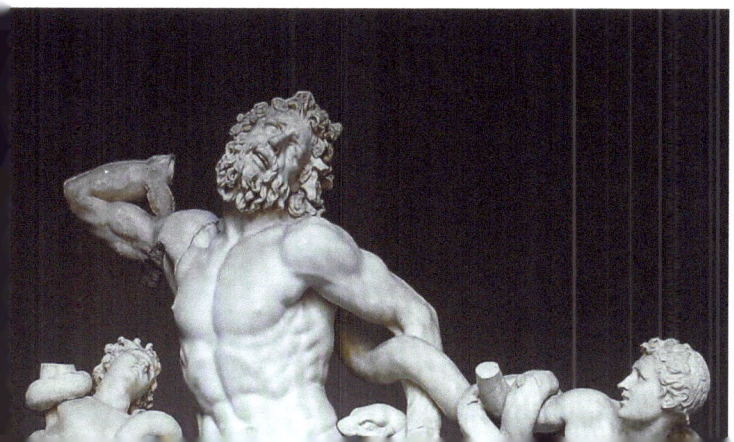

isn't my ass beautiful ! *kill the priest !* 21

yes   *kill the priest !*

kill the priest

let the selfie in

kill!

aren't we beautiful !

yes   *kill!*

kill the priest

let the selfie in   *kill !*

kill!

kill the priest   *kill the priest !*

if you want my ass

kill the priest if you like my ass

kill the priest
kill the priest   aren't we Beautiful !

kill the priest !

let the selfie in

isn't my ass Beautiful !

isn't my ass beautiful ! *kill the priest !*

yes

kill the priest

let the selfie in   *Crawl !*

kill!

aren't we beautiful !

yes   *kill!*

kill the priest

let the selfie in   *kill !*

aren't we Beautiful !   *kill!*

kill the priest   *kill the priest !*

kill !   *Kill!*

if you want my ass

kill the priest if you like my ass

kill the priest
kill the priest   *yes !* *kill!*   *kill!*
kill the priest !

01001O1 1OOIOOI OIIIOOI 1O1OOOI OOOO1O1

The Unveiling of The Selfie

(1010000 1000101 1001110 100101 1010011 = PENIS / 1010011 1000101 1001100 100 0110 1001001 1000101 = SELFIE)

celebrations around

e e cummings

44

the boys i mean are too refined
they go with girls in pink and white
they swipe their phones and pray for luck
they wet themselves to sleep at night

one hangs a ring upon her tit
one paints a cross in her behind
they shit to eat and worship wit
the boys i mean are too refined

they come with girls in cap and gown
who read in tweet and write in rhyme
who laugh to spite and fuck to live
and masturbate with toys at night

the boys i mean are too refined
they chat of this and nod to that
they speak of art
and live to piss

they speak whatever's in your mind
they kiss whatever's in your pants
the boys i mean are too refined
they shake like zombies when they dance

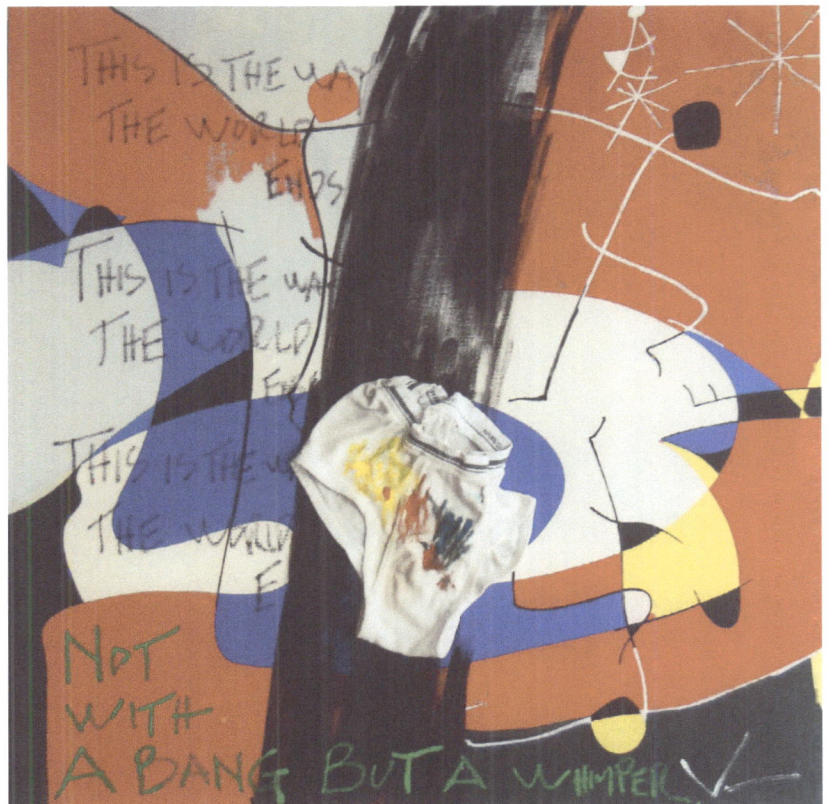

the boys i mean are not refined
they go with girls who buck and bite
they do not give a fuck for luck
they hump them thirteen times a night

one hangs a hat upon her tit
one carves a cross in her behind
they do not give a shit for wit
the boys i mean are not refined

they come with girls who bite and buck
who cannot read and cannot write
who laugh like they would fall apart
and masturbate with dynamite

the boys i mean are not refined
they cannot chat of that and this
they do not give a fart for art
they kill like you would take a piss

they speak whatever's on their mind
they do whatever's in their pants
the boys i mean are not refined
they shake the mountains when they dance

44

e e cummings

Celebrations Around Town

Carretadas al cementerio.

Left, Right   Left, Right
Left, Right
Left, Right   Left, Right

It's twelve midnight   Left, Right   Left, Right   Left, Right
and all is right   Left, Right   Left, Right   Left, Right
Left, Right It's all good   Left, Right   Left, Right   Left, Right
Left, Right   Left, Right   Left, Right   and all is right
Left, Right   and all is right   It's twelve o'clock
It's all good   Left, Right   It's twelve o'clock

all is right   Left, Right   **It's twelve midnight** Left, Right
Left, Right   Left, Right   **and all is right** Left, Right
Left, Right   Left, Right   Left, Right
Left, Right   Left, Right   Left, Right
Left, Right   Left, Right   Left, Right
Left, Right   Left, Right   Left, Right
Left, Right   Left, Right   Left, Right
Left, Right   Left, Right   Left, Right
Left, Right   Left, Right   Left, Right
Left, Right   Left, Right   Left, Right
and all is right   Left, Right   Left, Right
It's twelve o'clock   Left, Right

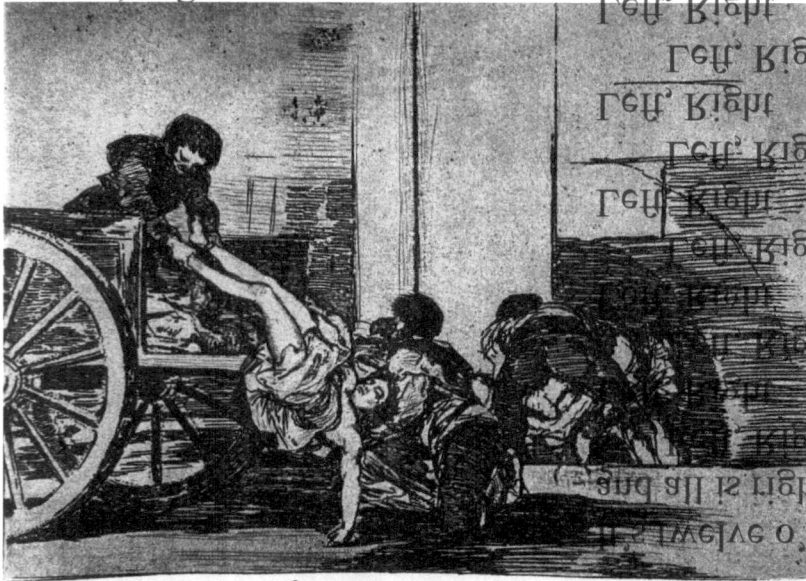

Carretadas al cementerio.

It's twelve midnight   Left, Right   Left, Right   Left, Right
and all is right   Left, Right   Left, Right   Left, Right
Left, Right It's all good   Left, Right   Left, Right   Left, Right
Left, Right   Left, Right   Left, Right   and all is right
Left, Right   and all is right   It's twelve o'clock
It's all good   Left, Right   It's twelve o'clock

all is right   Left, Right   **It's twelve midnight** Left, Right
Left, Right   Left, Right   **and all is right** Left, Right
Left, Right   Left, Right   Left, Right
Left, Right   Left, Right   Left, Right
Left, Right   Left, Right   Left, Right
Left, Right   Left, Right   Left, Right
Left, Right   Left, Right   Left, Right

Requiem

Requiem

Grant them eternal rest, O Lord, and let perpetual light shine upon them

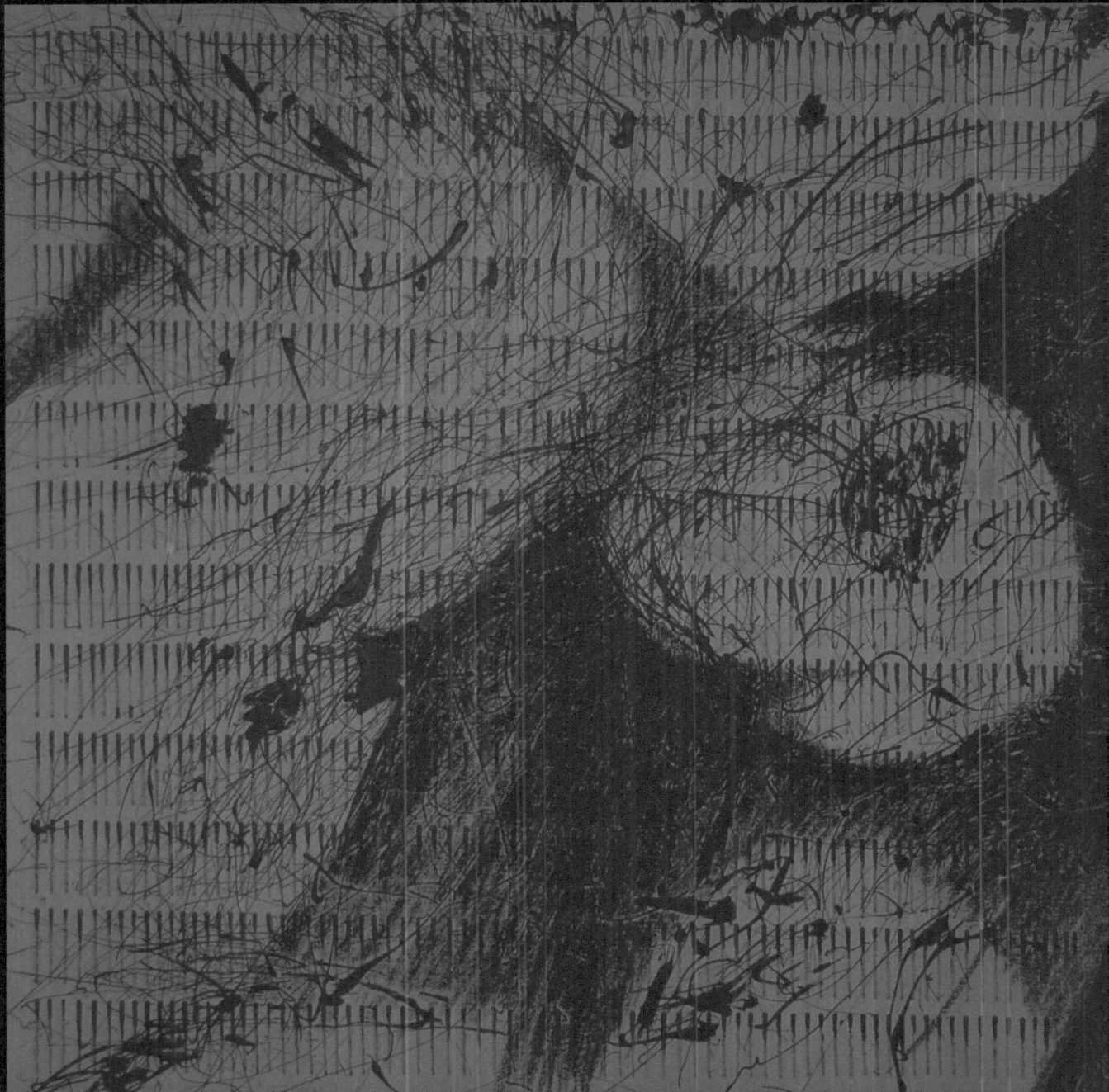

Dies irae ! dies illa ! Solvet saeclum in favilla: Teste David cum Sibylla !

Day of wrath ! O day of mourning ! O day of mourning ! See fulfilled the profets' warning, Heaven and earth in ashes burning

Libera me, Domine,
de morte aeterna,
in die illa tremenda:
Quando coeli movendi
sunt et terra

Deliver me, O Lord
from death eternal
on that fearful day
When the heavens
and the earth
shall be moved

31

In local news: a new star will be dedicated on the Hollywood Walk of Fame

32
do coffee coffee coffee Starbucks
a local homeless man was found dead in front of a Fire Station in DTLA

to do
it's another sunny day in California.

to do
to do
my bra !
No bra !
No bra
no bra !
Stay tuned for the latest updates in traffic weather and sports. a bra
do to do to do no bra ! do a
to do do to do to do
I want no bra

Now back to our panel of experts on the latest celebrity sightings !
it

The *Morning News* coffee coffee **the**
latest
In other news: the White House announced the unemployment rate increased **outbreaks**

there I want I like **of schizophrenia** do to do to do to do I like
will be an want **for** like I want
up-surge **seem to be concentrated** fin **in depth** my shoes
ƒ troops to ish **news** COFFEE !
sent around art galleries your **&** COFFEE !
finish break COFFEE ! COFFEE !
to Iraq your breakfast **on both coasts:** fast 1000011 1001111 1000110 100 0110 1000101 1000101
a Where MORNING **New York** it 00111 **expert analysis**
are my COFFEE with a VIEW 's **follow us on**
White House 1001101 1001111 1010010 100111 **and now** time **Twitter**
shoes to
spokesman drink **L.A.** go I don't wannaaa
I want up pull up your pants !
said your tuck in your shirt
milk ! I don't like it put on your shoes ! *hold the milk* ! coffee
today y're late for school I don't wannaaa ! caffe macchiato !
caffe latte !
tall cappuccino !

In local news: a new star will be dedicated on the Hollywood Walk of Fame
do coffee coffee coffee Starbucks
a local homeless man was found dead in front of a Fire Station in DTLA
to do
to do **it's another sunny day in California.**
my bra ! No bra !
No bra
no bra !
Stay tuned for the latest updates in traffic weather and sports. a bra
do to do no bra ! do a
to do do to do to do
I want no bra

Now back to our panel of experts on the latest celebrity sightings !
it

The *Morning News* coffee coffee **the**
latest
In other news: the White House announced the unemployment rate increased
there **outbreaks**
will be an I I like **of schizophrenia** do to do to do to do I like
up-surge want **for** like I want
of troops **seem to be concentrated** fin **in depth** my shoes
to ish **news** COFFEE !
around art galleries your **&** COFFEE !
break **COFFEE !**
on both coasts: fast 1111 1000110 100 0110 1000101 100010

Not That ! This !

Like

Afterword

It had been known, though there were no records, that K's executioners reported to the high Court that K had been reluctant to the end, and that he did not gracefully resign himself to the Court's verdict and that he did not kill himself as expected, and that they, the executioners, had to do the killing themselves. Nothing further was said, but a note was entered by the Judges in the Official Dossier and the case was closed . It had also been rumored, among the Court functionaries, that the Judges had not been pleased with the way K's case had been handled, there had been to much resistance on K's part, and that they wished for a better way to be found, one in which the accused would gracefully consent to and never challenge the Court's verdict in any way that was not intended by the Court.

Now, in 2100, some 175 years after Kafka's novel *The Trial* had first been published, the director for cultural studies at the Museum of Anthropology for the New North American Territories wondered if the artifacts he was receiving on a regular basis, might be the work of Titorelli's descendants; after all the position of Court Painter had been an inherited position, still was, and the Court Painters were among the few who knew the unspoken whishes of the Judges. In reviewing K's Trial, he also remembered that K had purchased three paintings from Titorelli, all identical.

The director wandered if these had anything to do with the *"Like"* computer buttons he was getting at the same time and from the same places in the now deserted North American cities. He decided to store them in a special room until he could decide what he connection was. He then had his assistants come up with an bstraction in drawing form for the generating concept of these artifacts and had the drawing posted on the door to the room.

The drawing has since been referred to as the " *The Stamp* ", and is reproduced below.

Not That !   This !

VB

BINARY CONVERSIONS

1000011 1001111 1000110 1000110 1000101   C O F F E

1000011 1010010 1000001 1010111 1001100   C R A W L

1001011 1001001 1001100 100 1100   K I L L

1001101 1001111 1010010 1001110 1001001 1001110 1000111   M O R N I N G

1010000 1000101 1001110 1001001 1010011   P E N I S

1010000 1001001 1010011 1010011   P I S S

1010011 1000101 1001100 1000110 1001001 1000101   S E L F I E

1010111 1001001 1010100 1010100 1011001   W I T T Y

0100001   !

References and Illustration Credits

These are the artists whose work I incorporated and / or made reference to throughout this book. I certainly hope that their names and works require no introduction and that they were recognized by the reader at first sight. Here they are listed in the order of their appearance together with the source material and / or the location from which I reproduced their work.

page 3   *Francisco Goya : The Hardship of Old Age* / Brown Ink Wash -Drawing / Prado Museum, Madrid

page 7   *Constantin Brancusi : The Cock* / Wild Cherry Sculpture
photograph reproduced from "Constantine Brancusi" published by the Philadelphia Museum of Art
Copyright @ 1995 Philadelphia Museum of Art.
All rights reserved @ 1995 Estate of Constantin Brancusi / Artists Rights Society (ARS) New York

pages 9 and 31   *Alberto Giacometti : Walking Man 1* / Bronze Sculpture / Carnegie Museum of Art, Pittsburgh

page 13   *Paul Klee : The Eye* / Pastel on jute-Painting
photograph reproduced from "Paul Klee Notebooks Volume 1-The Thinking Eye"
published by Lund Humphries Publishers Limited. Copyright @ 1961 Lund Humphries, London

     Andy Warhol : Campbell's Soup / screen print

page 15   *Igor Stravinsky : The Rite of Spring* / photographic reproduction of music score,
photograph (The Kiss of the Earth / The Dancing Out of the Earth) , reproduced from
" Igor Stravinsky-The Rite of Spring" published by Dover Publications. Copyright @ 1989 by Dover Publications, Inc.

page 16   *Albert Giraud : Mondestrunken (Drunk with Moonlight)* / Poem from "Pierrot Lunaire"
English translation by Stanley Appelbaum

page 17   *Arnold Schoenberg: Pierrot Lunaire, Op. 21* / photographic reproduction of music score,
photograph (1. Mondestrunken) , reproduced from " Arnold Schoenberg-Verklarte Nacht and Pierrot Lunaire"
published by Dover Publications. Copyright @ 1994 by Dover Publications, Inc

page 21   *Laocoon and his Sons* / Marble Sculpture / Vatican Museum , Vatican City-Rome

page 23   *E.E. Cummings : The boys I mean are not refined* / Poem from the "No Thanks" collection
reproduced from E.E. Cummings Complete Poems 1904-1962 edited by George James Firmage
published by Liveright Publishing Corporation. Copyright @ 1935 by E.E. Cummings,
Copyright @ 1968 by Marion Morehouse Cummings, Copyright @ 1973, 1978 by George James Firmage
Copyright @ 1973, 1978 by the Trustees for the E.E. Cummings Trust,

page 24   *Francisco Goya : The Disasters of War* / *Plate 64-Cartloads for the cemetery,*
photograph reproduced from " The Disasters of War " by Francisco Goya , published by Dover Publications
Copyright @ 1967 by Dover Publications, Inc.

page 25   *Francisco Goya : The 3rd of May 1808* / Oil Painting / Prado Museum, Madrid

page 26   *Francisco Goya : The Disasters of War* / *Plate 72-The Consequences*
photograph reproduced from " The Disasters of War" by Francisco Goya, published by Dover Publications
Copyright @ 1967 by Dover Publications, Inc.

pages 30,31   *Giuseppe Verdi : Requiem* / photographic reproduction of music score,
photograph (Nr. 7. Libera me), reproduced from " Giuseppe Verdi-Requiem", published by Dover Publications

The illustrations on the book covers and on pages iv, vi, 5, 11, 15, 17, 19, 22, 23, 27, 28, 29, 30, 31 and 33 are from my own paintings and digital works.